Chimichanga Creations

A Flavorful Journey into Mexican Cuisine

While every precaution has been taken in the preparation of this book, the publisher assumes no responsibility for errors or omissions, or for damages resulting from the use of the information contained herein.

CHIMICHANGA CREATIONS

First edition. December 18, 2023.

Copyright © 2023 Jose Maria.

ISBN: 979-8223768890

Written by Jose Maria.

Table of Contents

Jose Maria

❖ Introduction

A. Brief History of Chimichangas

Chimichangas have a fascinating history that traces back to the southwestern regions of the United States and Mexico. The exact origin remains a subject of debate, with various claims attributing its creation to different places. One popular tale suggests that the dish was an accidental creation when a burrito was dropped into a deep fryer, resulting in the crispy and golden delicacy we now know as the chimichanga.

B. Significance in Mexican Cuisine

Chimichangas have become a beloved and iconic dish, symbolizing the rich tapestry of Mexican cuisine. Their popularity extends beyond borders, captivating taste buds worldwide. In Mexican culture, chimichangas are often associated with festive occasions and family gatherings, bringing people together over a shared love for these delicious, deep-fried parcels of flavor.

C. Key Ingredients Overview

To embark on the journey of creating authentic chimichangas, it's essential to acquaint ourselves with the key ingredients that contribute to their distinctive taste and texture:

- **Flour Tortillas:** The foundation of a good chimichanga, providing a soft interior and becoming delightfully crispy when fried.
- **Shredded Chicken or Beef:** A succulent and flavorful protein base, often seasoned with traditional Mexican spices to enhance the overall taste.
- **Beans:** Whether black or pinto, beans add a hearty and nutritious element to the filling.
- **Cheese:** A melty, gooey component that binds the ingredients

together and contributes to the richness of the dish.

- **Authentic Mexican Spices:** A blend of cumin, chili powder, garlic, and other spices that infuse the filling with the bold and aromatic flavors characteristic of Mexican cuisine.

As we delve deeper into the world of chimichangas, these key ingredients will harmonize to create a culinary masterpiece that pays homage to the vibrant and diverse tapestry of Mexican flavors.

Chapter(1) Kitchen Essentials

A. Tools and Utensils

1. Deep Fryer or Heavy-Bottomed Pan:

To achieve that perfect golden-brown crispiness, a deep fryer is ideal. Alternatively, a heavy-bottomed pan with enough oil for submersion can be used.

2. Tongs:

Essential for carefully flipping and retrieving the chimichangas from the hot oil to ensure an even fry.

3. Paper Towels:

Place them on a plate to absorb excess oil, keeping the chimichangas crispy without being greasy.

B. Essential Ingredients

1. Oil for Frying:

Choose a high-smoke-point oil like vegetable or canola to ensure the chimichangas cook evenly without imparting unwanted flavors.

2. Salsa and Guacamole for Serving:

These fresh and vibrant accompaniments enhance the chimichanga experience, providing a burst of flavors. Consider preparing homemade salsa and guacamole for an authentic touch.

C. Tips for Success

1. Ensure Tortillas are Room Temperature:

Cold tortillas are prone to cracking. Allow them to reach room temperature before assembling to ensure they remain pliable and fold easily.

2. Properly Seal the Edges:

When filling and folding the chimichangas, ensure a tight seal to prevent the filling from escaping during frying.

3. Maintain Consistent Oil Temperature:

Keep the oil temperature around 350-375°F (175-190°C) for optimal frying. This ensures a quick and even cook, resulting in a crispy exterior.

4. Avoid Overcrowding the Fryer:

Fry chimichangas in batches to maintain the oil temperature. Overcrowding can lead to uneven cooking and a less-than-crispy texture.

5. Experiment with Filling Combinations:

While the classic recipe is timeless, don't be afraid to experiment with different protein options, spice levels, and additional fillings to personalize your chimichangas.

6. Serve Immediately:

Chimichangas are at their best when served hot and fresh. Enjoy them immediately with salsa and guacamole for a delightful culinary experience.

By following these kitchen essentials and tips, you'll be well-prepared to embark on the flavorful journey of crafting the perfect chimichanga.

Chapter(2) Classic Chimichanga Recipe

A. Traditional Filling Options

1. Shredded Chicken:

Cook boneless, skinless chicken breasts or thighs with traditional Mexican spices such as cumin, chili powder, garlic powder, and oregano until fully cooked and easily shredded.

2. Beef Barbacoa:

Slow-cook beef chuck with adobo sauce, chipotle peppers, and a blend of spices until tender. Shred the beef for a rich and flavorful filling.

3. Bean and Cheese:

Combine refried beans with shredded cheese (like cheddar or Monterey Jack) for a vegetarian option that doesn't compromise on taste.

B. Authentic Seasoning Techniques

1. Mexican Spice Blend:

Mix ground cumin, chili powder, garlic powder, onion powder, oregano, and a pinch of cayenne for an authentic and robust seasoning.

2. Marinating Meats:

For meat fillings, marinate the proteins in lime juice, minced garlic, and the spice blend for at least 30 minutes to infuse them with bold flavors.

C. Step-by-Step Assembly Guide

1. Prepare the Tortillas:

Warm the tortillas to make them pliable. You can do this on a dry skillet or microwave them for a few seconds.

2. Add the Filling:

Place a generous portion of the chosen filling in the center of each tortilla, leaving space around the edges.

3. Fold and Seal:

Fold the sides of the tortilla toward the center, then fold the top and bottom to create a rectangular parcel. Use toothpicks if needed to secure the edges.

4. Properly Seal the Edges:

Ensure a tight seal to prevent the filling from leaking during frying. Press the edges firmly together.

D. Proper Frying Tips

1. Oil Temperature:

Maintain the oil temperature between 350-375°F (175-190°C). This ensures a quick fry, sealing the tortilla and creating a crispy exterior.

2. Careful Submersion:

Gently place the chimichangas into the hot oil using tongs. Avoid splashing to prevent burns.

3. Even Cooking:

Fry the chimichangas for 3-4 minutes per side, or until they achieve a golden-brown color. Turn them carefully with tongs to ensure even cooking.

4. Draining Excess Oil:

Once fried, place the chimichangas on a plate lined with paper towels to absorb excess oil. Pat them gently to maintain crispiness.

5. Serve Immediately:

The classic chimichangas are at their best when served immediately. Accompany them with fresh salsa and guacamole for a burst of flavor.

By following these steps, you'll create classic chimichangas with a crispy exterior and a flavorful, well-seasoned filling that pays homage to the heart of Mexican cuisine.

Chapter(3) Creative Variations

A. Seafood Chimichanga

1. Shrimp and Crab Filling:

Sauté shrimp and crab meat with garlic, lime juice, and a touch of cayenne for a zesty seafood filling.

2. Fresh Salsa Verde:

Top the seafood chimichangas with a vibrant salsa verde made from tomatillos, green onions, cilantro, and lime juice.

3. Cilantro-Lime Crema:

Drizzle a cilantro-lime crema over the chimichangas for added freshness. Combine sour cream, lime juice, chopped cilantro, and a pinch of salt.

B. Vegetarian Delights

1. Roasted Vegetable Medley:

Roast a mix of bell peppers, onions, zucchini, and corn with olive oil and taco seasoning for a flavorful vegetarian filling.

2. Black Bean and Corn Salsa:

Mix black beans, corn, diced tomatoes, red onion, and cilantro for a refreshing salsa to accompany the vegetarian chimichangas.

3. Avocado-Lime Sauce:

Blend ripe avocados with lime juice, garlic, and a hint of cumin to create a creamy and tangy sauce for topping.

C. Fusion Flavors

1. Korean BBQ Beef:

Marinate beef in a Korean BBQ sauce and cook until tender. Use this as the filling for a unique fusion chimichanga.

2. Kimchi Slaw:

Top the Korean BBQ chimichangas with a slaw made from shredded cabbage, carrots, and kimchi for a spicy kick.

3. Sriracha-Lime Drizzle:

Create a spicy sriracha-lime drizzle by mixing sriracha sauce with lime juice. Drizzle it over the fusion chimichangas for an extra layer of flavor.

D. Breakfast Chimichangas

1. Scrambled Egg Filling:

Scramble eggs with sautéed onions, bell peppers, and your choice of breakfast sausage or bacon.

2. Cheese and Salsa Fresca:

Add a blend of cheeses and top the breakfast chimichangas with a fresh salsa fresca made from diced tomatoes, onions, cilantro, and lime juice.

3. Avocado-Cilantro Cream:

Create a creamy topping by blending avocados with cilantro, sour cream, and a squeeze of lime for a breakfast chimichanga delight.

Experimenting with these creative variations allows you to explore different flavor profiles and make chimichangas suitable for various occasions and preferences.

Chapter(4) Sides and Accompaniments

A. Salsa and Guacamole Recipes

1. Classic Tomato Salsa:

Ingredients:

- Diced tomatoes
- Red onions
- Fresh cilantro
- Jalapeños (seeds removed for milder salsa)
- Lime juice
- Salt and pepper to taste

2. Zesty Guacamole:

Ingredients:

- Ripe avocados
- Red onion, finely diced
- Fresh cilantro, chopped
- Jalapeño, finely minced
- Lime juice
- Salt and cumin to taste

3. Mango-Pineapple Salsa:

Ingredients:

- Diced mango
- Diced pineapple
- Red bell pepper, finely chopped
- Red onion, minced
- Fresh mint leaves, chopped
- Lime juice
- Salt to taste

B. Perfect Rice and Beans Pairings

1. Cilantro-Lime Rice:

Fluff white rice and fold in chopped cilantro and a squeeze of lime juice for a fragrant and citrusy rice.

2. Black Beans with Garlic and Cumin:

Sauté black beans with minced garlic, cumin, and a pinch of salt for a flavorful and hearty bean accompaniment.

3. Mexican Street Corn Salad:

Combine grilled corn kernels with mayonnaise, cotija cheese, lime juice, and chili powder for a delectable side dish.

C. Refreshing Salad Combinations

1. Cucumber and Tomato Salad:

Toss cucumber slices, cherry tomatoes, red onion, and fresh cilantro with olive oil, red wine vinegar, and salt for a crisp and refreshing salad.

2. Avocado and Black Bean Salad:

Mix diced avocados, black beans, corn, red onion, and lime vinaigrette for a colorful and nutritious salad.

3. Jicama and Mango Slaw:

Shred jicama and mango into thin strips, add shredded cabbage, and toss with lime juice, honey, and a pinch of salt for a crunchy and tropical slaw.

These vibrant and flavorful sides complement the chimichangas perfectly, offering a balance of textures and tastes that elevate the entire dining experience.

Chapter(5) Healthier Alternatives

A. Baked Chimichangas

1. Baked Chicken Chimichangas:

- Lightly brush tortillas with olive oil.
- Fill with seasoned shredded chicken, beans, and a modest amount of cheese.
- Place seam side down on a baking sheet.
- Bake at 375°F (190°C) for 20-25 minutes until golden and crisp.

2. Vegetarian Baked Chimichangas:

- Use a mix of roasted vegetables, black beans, and reduced-fat cheese as the filling.
- Brush tortillas with olive oil and bake until crispy and browned.

3. Baked Seafood Chimichangas:

- Create a filling with shrimp and crab, seasoned with lime and spices.
- Bake until the tortillas are golden, delivering a healthier alternative to the traditional fried version.

B. Lean Protein Options

1. Turkey Picadillo Filling:

Cook ground turkey with tomatoes, onions, garlic, and a blend of spices for a lean and flavorful filling.

2. Grilled Chicken Breast Filling:

Grill chicken breasts with a smoky chipotle marinade for a lean and protein-packed option.

3. Lean Beef and Bean Filling:

Combine lean ground beef with black beans and a variety of spices for a satisfying and nutritious chimichanga filling.

C. Whole Grain Wrappers

1. Whole Wheat Tortillas:

Opt for whole wheat tortillas to increase fiber content and enhance the nutritional profile of your chimichangas.

2. Quinoa and Brown Rice Filling:

Mix cooked quinoa and brown rice with your choice of lean protein and vegetables for a wholesome and filling option.

3. Multi-Grain Blend:

Explore tortillas made from a blend of whole grains, such as whole wheat, corn, and oats, for added texture and nutritional benefits.

These healthier alternatives provide options for those seeking lighter, nutrient-dense versions of the classic chimichanga while still savoring the delicious flavors of Mexican cuisine.

Chapter(6) Serving and Presentation

A. Plating Suggestions

1. Individual Plating:

Place a chimichanga on a plate at a slight angle, allowing the crispy golden exterior to showcase. Spoon a generous portion of salsa and guacamole on the side.

2. Chimichanga Tower:

Arrange two or three chimichangas vertically, creating a tower effect. Drizzle salsa and guacamole down the sides for an artistic presentation.

3. Overlapping Presentation:

Overlap two chimichangas on the plate for an elegant and visually appealing arrangement. Garnish with a sprig of fresh cilantro.

B. Garnishing Techniques

1. Fresh Herb Sprinkle:

Sprinkle finely chopped fresh cilantro or parsley over the chimichangas just before serving to add a burst of color and freshness.

2. Lime Wedge Accent:

Place a lime wedge on the plate to add a citrusy element. Squeeze it over the chimichanga just before indulging for a burst of flavor.

3. Radish Roses:

Create delicate radish roses as a garnish. Slice radishes thinly, then fan out the slices to resemble roses, placing them beside the chimichanga.

C. Family-Style Serving Ideas

1. Chimichanga Platter:

Arrange a variety of chimichangas on a large platter for a colorful display. Surround them with bowls of different salsas and guacamoles for a communal dining experience.

2. Build-Your-Own Chimichanga Bar:

Set up a station with a variety of fillings, tortillas, and toppings. Let family and guests assemble their chimichangas according to their preferences.

3. Chimichanga Buffet:

Create a buffet-style spread with a selection of chimichangas, sides, and accompaniments. This allows everyone to customize their plate based on their taste.

These serving and presentation ideas add a touch of flair to your chimichanga experience, making the meal not only delicious but visually enticing as well. Whether plated individually or served family-style, these techniques enhance the overall dining enjoyment.

Chapter(7) Troubleshooting Guide

A. Common Mistakes and How to Avoid Them
 1. Cracked Tortillas:

- **Avoidance:** Ensure tortillas are at room temperature before filling to prevent cracking.

- **Solution:** If a tortilla cracks, warm it slightly in the microwave or on a dry skillet to restore pliability.

2. Filling Spillage During Frying:

- **Avoidance:** Properly seal the chimichanga edges before frying.
- **Solution:** Use toothpicks to secure edges, or fold the tortilla more tightly to prevent filling leakage.

3. Soggy Chimichangas:

- **Avoidance:** Ensure oil is at the correct temperature before frying.
- **Solution:** If chimichangas are soggy, increase oil temperature and fry for an additional minute on each side.

4. Unevenly Cooked Chimichangas:

- **Avoidance:** Fry chimichangas in batches to prevent overcrowding.
- **Solution:** Turn chimichangas carefully with tongs for even cooking. Adjust oil temperature if needed.

B. Substitution Options
1. Tortilla Substitutes:

- **Corn Tortillas:** Substitute flour tortillas with corn tortillas for a gluten-free alternative.
- **Whole Wheat Tortillas:** Opt for whole wheat tortillas for added fiber and nutrients.

2. Protein Substitutes:

- **Tofu:** Use crumbled and seasoned tofu as a plant-based protein option.

- **Ground Turkey:** Replace ground beef with lean ground turkey for a lighter filling.

3. Cheese Options:

- **Reduced-Fat Cheese:** Choose reduced-fat versions or use smaller amounts for a healthier option.
- **Queso Fresco:** Use crumbled queso fresco for a lighter, tangy alternative.

C. Handling Leftovers
1. Reheating Chimichangas:

- **Oven Method:** Preheat the oven to 350°F (175°C) and bake chimichangas for about 10-15 minutes until heated through.
- **Pan Method:** Reheat in a pan over medium heat with a bit of oil, turning occasionally until crispy.

2. Refreshing Sides:

- **Salsa and Guacamole:** Freshen up salsa with additional lime juice, and guacamole with a sprinkle of salt before serving leftovers.

3. Creative Repurposing:

- **Chimichanga Bowl:** Deconstruct chimichangas and serve the filling over rice or salad for a different presentation.

- Chimichanga Quesadilla: Use the filling to make a quick and flavorful quesadilla.

By addressing common mistakes, offering substitution options, and providing tips for handling leftovers, this troubleshooting guide ensures a smoother chimichanga cooking experience and helps make the most of any culinary challenges.

Chapter(8) Expert Tips from Mexican Chefs

A. Insightful Advice
1. Balance of Flavors:

- **Expert Tip:** Chef's advice emphasizes achieving a harmonious balance of flavors. Ensure that your chimichanga filling strikes a perfect balance between savory, spicy, and tangy elements.

2. Authenticity Matters:

- **Expert Tip:** Mexican chefs stress the importance of using authentic Mexican spices and ingredients. Seek out quality, traditional ingredients for an authentic chimichanga experience.

3. Freshness is Key:

- **Expert Tip:** Emphasize the use of fresh herbs and produce. Fresh cilantro, tomatoes, and lime juice can elevate the overall taste and provide a burst of freshness.

B. Secret Ingredients
1. Mexican Oregano:

- **Expert Insight:** Mexican chefs often use Mexican oregano for its distinct flavor. Add a pinch to your spice blend for an authentic touch.

2. Achiote Paste:

- **Expert Insight:** Achiote paste, made from annatto seeds, lends a unique color and earthy flavor. It's a secret ingredient for some chefs, especially in meat marinades.

3. Epazote Herb:

- **Expert Insight:** For an extra layer of authenticity, consider using epazote. This herb has a distinct flavor and is commonly used in Mexican cooking, particularly with bean dishes.

C. Personal Touches
1. Handmade Tortillas:

- **Expert Insight:** Some chefs advocate for handmade tortillas for an added level of authenticity. If time allows, consider crafting your own tortillas for a personal touch.

2. Custom Spice Blends:

- **Expert Insight:** Experiment with creating your spice blends. While there are traditional recipes, adding your unique twist can make the dish truly yours.

3. Family Recipes:

- **Expert Insight:** Incorporate family recipes or personal touches passed down through generations. It's these small details that can make your chimichangas extra special.

These expert tips from Mexican chefs offer valuable insights, secret ingredients, and personal touches that can elevate your chimichanga creations to an authentic and memorable culinary experience.

Chapter(9) Chimichanga Celebrations

A. Festive Occasions to Serve Chimichangas

1. Cinco de Mayo Fiesta:

Celebrate the vibrant flavors of Mexico on Cinco de Mayo by serving a spread of chimichangas with a variety of fillings, accompanied by margaritas and traditional Mexican music.

2. Birthday Bash:

Customize chimichangas with the birthday person's favorite fillings and host a chimichanga-themed birthday party. Consider creating a chimichanga bar for guests to assemble their own.

3. Game Day Gathering:

Make chimichangas the star of your game day spread. Prepare an assortment of fillings, and serve with refreshing beverages for a flavorful game-watching experience.

B. Customizing for Special Events

1. Wedding Celebrations:

Offer a unique and memorable menu by incorporating chimichangas into wedding celebrations. Consider a variety of fillings and elegant presentation for a festive touch.

2. Anniversary Dinner:

Celebrate milestones with a romantic chimichanga dinner. Customize the fillings to reflect the couple's favorite flavors and serve with a side of Mexican wine or sangria.

3. Holiday Feasts:

Add a Mexican flair to holiday celebrations by including chimichangas in your feast. Consider festive fillings and garnishes to suit the holiday theme.

C. Hosting a Chimichanga Party

1. Chimichanga Bar:

Set up a chimichanga bar with various fillings, sauces, and toppings. Let guests assemble their chimichangas for a personalized dining experience.

2. Chimichanga Contest:

Host a chimichanga-making contest at your party. Provide different fillings and let guests get creative. Award prizes for the most delicious and inventive chimichangas.

3. Mexican Fiesta Decor:

Decorate your space with vibrant colors, sombreros, and festive banners to create a lively Mexican fiesta atmosphere. Play traditional music to enhance the experience.

Chimichangas can add a flavorful and festive touch to a variety of celebrations. Whether it's a special occasion, a themed party, or a casual gathering, incorporating chimichangas into your menu can make the event truly memorable.

Chapter(10) Advanced Flavor Profiles

A. Exploring Regional Variations
  1. Sonoran Style:

- **Flavor Profile:** Sonoran chimichangas often feature beef fillings with a blend of spices like cumin and coriander. Served with a side of pickled vegetables for a tangy kick.

2. Baja California Twist:

- **Flavor Profile:** Baja-style chimichangas may incorporate seafood like shrimp or fish. Complemented by a fresh mango salsa and a drizzle of chipotle aioli for a coastal influence.

3. Oaxacan Inspiration:

- **Flavor Profile:** Oaxacan chimichangas might include mole sauce and shredded chicken, creating a rich and complex flavor profile. Garnish with crumbled queso fresco and chopped cilantro.

B. Unique Spices and Seasonings
1. Ancho Chili Rub:

- **Flavor Boost:** Create a rub using ground ancho chili, smoked paprika, and a touch of cinnamon for a smoky, slightly sweet, and spicy flavor.

2. Adobo Marinade:

- **Flavor Boost:** Marinate meats in an adobo sauce made from dried chilies, garlic, oregano, and vinegar for a bold and tangy taste.

3. Citrus Zest Infusion:

- **Flavor Boost:** Add zest from oranges or limes to the filling for a citrusy lift that enhances the overall brightness of the chimichangas.

C. Incorporating Indigenous Ingredients
1. Nopales (Cactus Paddles):

- **Ingredient Incorporation:** Include diced and sautéed nopales in the filling for a unique texture and a nod to indigenous Mexican ingredients.

2. Huitlacoche (Corn Smut):

- **Ingredient Incorporation**: Consider incorporating huitlacoche, a corn fungus with an earthy and savory flavor, into vegetarian chimichangas for a distinctive twist.

3. Achiote Seeds:

- **Ingredient Incorporation:** Infuse the filling with achiote seeds for a warm, peppery flavor and a vibrant red hue. Achiote is commonly used in indigenous Mexican cuisine.

Exploring regional variations, incorporating unique spices, and using indigenous ingredients can elevate chimichangas to an advanced level of culinary artistry, allowing for a deeper appreciation of the diverse and rich tapestry of Mexican flavors.

Chapter(11) Family Recipes and Traditions

A. Passed-Down Chimichanga Secrets
1. Grandma's Special Spice Blend:

- **Cherished Secret:** Many families have a special spice blend passed down through generations. Whether it's a unique combination of cumin, coriander, or a secret chili powder mix, these blends are a closely guarded secret.

2. Matriarch's Frying Techniques:

- **Cherished Secret:** The matriarch of the family often imparts her wisdom on the art of frying chimichangas. From achieving the perfect crispiness to the ideal frying temperature, these techniques are invaluable.

3. Secret Family Sauce:

- **Cherished Secret:** Families may have a secret sauce, whether it's a special salsa, guacamole, or chimichanga dressing. These secret recipes add a personal touch that makes each chimichanga unique.

B. Stories Behind Generational Variations
1. Evolution of Fillings:

- **Generational Shift:** Families may have witnessed a shift in chimichanga fillings over the years. From traditional beef to modern seafood or vegetarian options, each generation adds its own twist.

2. Incorporating Global Influences:

- **Generational Shift:** With globalization, families may introduce international flavors into chimichangas. Whether it's a fusion of Mexican and Asian influences or a Mediterranean twist, these variations tell a story of cultural exchange.

3. Adapting to Dietary Preferences:

- **Generational Shift:** Families often adapt chimichanga recipes to meet changing dietary preferences. Whether it's creating gluten-free versions or exploring plant-based options, these adaptations reflect a commitment to inclusivity.

C. Preserving Culinary Heritage
1. Cooking Together:

- **Culinary Bonding:** Families preserve their culinary heritage by cooking together. Passing down chimichanga recipes involves hands-on experience, storytelling, and a sense of shared tradition.

2. Recipe Journals and Cookbooks:

- **Documentation:** Many families maintain recipe journals or cookbooks that document the history and evolution of their chimichanga recipes. These become cherished family heirlooms.

3. Celebrating Food Rituals:

- **Generational Connection:** Families may have rituals associated with making and enjoying chimichangas. Whether it's a special occasion or a weekly tradition, these rituals help maintain a connection to cultural roots.

Family recipes and traditions surrounding chimichangas are not just about the food itself; they carry stories, memories, and a sense of identity. By preserving culinary heritage, families ensure that the art of making chimichangas continues to be a cherished and shared experience across generations.

Chapter(12) International Fusion

A. Asian-inspired Chimichangas
 1. Teriyaki Chicken Filling:

- **Inspiration:** Borrowing from Japanese cuisine, use teriyaki-marinated chicken as the filling for a sweet and savory twist.

2. Soy-Ginger Infusion:

- **Inspiration:** Incorporate a soy-ginger marinade for the protein filling, adding an Asian-inspired umami flavor to the chimichangas.

3. Wasabi Guacamole:

- **Inspiration:** Infuse guacamole with wasabi for a kick of heat and a unique Asian flavor that complements the traditional Mexican components.

B. Mediterranean Twists
1. Lamb and Feta Filling:

- **Inspiration:** Draw inspiration from Greek cuisine by using a filling of spiced lamb and crumbled feta for a Mediterranean flavor profile.

2. Tzatziki Drizzle:

- **Inspiration:** Instead of traditional sauces, drizzle chimichangas with a refreshing tzatziki sauce made from yogurt, cucumber, and mint.

3. Greek Salad Topping:

- **Inspiration:** Top chimichangas with a Greek salad mix of tomatoes, cucumbers, olives, and feta for a fresh and vibrant touch.

C. Global Influences on a Mexican Classic
1. Moroccan Spice Blend:

- **Influence:** Introduce Moroccan flavors by using a spice blend of cumin, coriander, cinnamon, and paprika for a fragrant and complex chimichanga filling.

2. Mango Chutney Drizzle:

- **Influence:** Add a touch of Indian cuisine by drizzling chimichangas with a sweet and tangy mango chutney for an unexpected burst of flavor.

3. Brazilian Black Bean Filling:

- **Influence:** Infuse chimichangas with a Brazilian twist by using a black bean and plantain filling seasoned with tropical spices like cayenne and lime.

Exploring international fusion with chimichangas allows for a creative blending of flavors from different culinary traditions. These inventive combinations showcase the versatility of this Mexican classic and open the door to a world of global influences on your plate.

Chapter(13) Gluten-Free and Dietary Considerations

A. Corn Tortilla Alternatives

1. Blue Corn Tortillas:

- **Gluten-Free Option:** Blue corn tortillas not only add a distinctive color but also provide a gluten-free alternative with a slightly nuttier flavor.

2. White Corn Tortillas:

- **Gluten-Free Option:** Traditional white corn tortillas are naturally gluten-free and can be used as a suitable alternative for those with gluten sensitivities.

3. Plantain Wrappers:

- **Gluten-Free Option:** Explore plantain wrappers as a creative and gluten-free alternative. Thinly sliced and lightly fried plantains can serve as a flavorful and unique wrapping.

B. Gluten-Free Filling Options

1. Quinoa and Black Bean Filling:

- **Gluten-Free Option:** Create a protein-packed and gluten-free filling using quinoa and black beans seasoned with Mexican spices.

2. Grilled Vegetable Medley:

- **Gluten-Free Option:** Roast a medley of gluten-free vegetables, such as bell peppers, zucchini, and eggplant, and use them as a flavorful filling.

3. Tofu and Veggie Stir-Fry:

- **Gluten-Free Option:** Sauté tofu with a variety of fresh vegetables for a plant-based and gluten-free chimichanga filling.

C. Adapting Chimichangas for Special Diets
1. Paleo-Friendly Options:

- **Adaptation:** For those following a Paleo diet, use almond flour or cassava flour tortillas and fill with Paleo-friendly ingredients like grilled meats, vegetables, and avocado.

2. Vegetarian and Vegan Adaptations:

- **Adaptation:** Offer vegetarian and vegan options by using plant-based proteins such as tofu, tempeh, or beans as the filling. Ensure sauces and seasonings are free from animal products.

3. Low-Carb Alternatives:

- **Adaptation:** Cater to low-carb diets by using lettuce wraps or large cabbage leaves as an alternative to traditional tortillas. Fill with lean proteins and low-carb vegetables.

Considering dietary restrictions and adapting chimichangas accordingly allows for inclusivity and ensures that this delicious Mexican dish can be enjoyed by a diverse range of individuals with various dietary considerations.

Chapter(14) Cocktail and Beverage Pairings

A. Margaritas and Tequila-based Drinks
1. Classic Margarita:

- **Pairing Notes:** The tangy and citrusy notes of a classic margarita complement the richness of chimichangas. The salt rim enhances the overall flavor experience.

2. Spicy Jalapeño Margarita:

- **Pairing Notes:** Add a kick to your margarita with fresh jalapeños. The heat contrasts well with the savory flavors of chimichangas.

3. Tequila Sunrise:

- **Pairing Notes:** The fruity and vibrant Tequila Sunrise, with its combination of orange juice, grenadine, and tequila, adds a refreshing element to the chimichanga experience.

B. Mexican-Inspired Mocktails
1. Hibiscus Agua Fresca:

- **Pairing Notes:** The floral and slightly tart notes of hibiscus agua fresca provide a non-alcoholic option that complements the spices in chimichangas.

2. Cucumber Lime Mint Cooler:

- **Pairing Notes:** This refreshing mocktail, made with cucumber, lime, and mint, offers a cool contrast to the warm and savory chimichangas.

3. Pineapple Jalapeño Sparkler:

- **Pairing Notes:** A mix of pineapple juice and a hint of jalapeño creates a lively and tropical mocktail that pairs well with the bold flavors of chimichangas.

C. Beer and Wine Recommendations
1. Mexican Lager or Pilsner:

- **Pairing Notes:** A light and crisp Mexican lager or pilsner complements the savory and slightly spicy elements of chimichangas.

2. Sauvignon Blanc:

- **Pairing Notes:** The citrusy and herbal notes of Sauvignon Blanc provide a refreshing contrast to the richness of chimichangas, especially those with seafood fillings.

3. Spicy Red Zinfandel:

- **Pairing Notes:** A spicy red Zinfandel works well with the bold flavors of chimichangas, especially those with beef or spicy fillings.

Pairing chimichangas with the right beverages enhances the overall dining experience, whether you prefer a classic margarita, a refreshing mocktail, or the perfect beer or wine to complement the flavors of this Mexican classic.

Chapter(15) Street Food Adventures

A. Recreating Authentic Street-Style Chimichangas
    1. Street-Style Frying Techniques:

- **Authenticity:** Emulate the street food experience by using traditional frying techniques. Achieve a perfect golden crispiness by ensuring the oil is hot and the chimichangas are cooked quickly.

2. Simple and Flavorful Fillings:

- **Authenticity:** Street-style chimichangas often feature simple yet flavorful fillings. Use well-seasoned meats, fresh vegetables, and classic spices for an authentic taste.

3. Serving with Street-Style Salsas:

- **Authenticity:** Pair your chimichangas with street-style salsas like pico de gallo, roasted tomato salsa, or pickled onions to capture the true essence of street food.

B. Exploring Local Street Food Markets
1. Market Research for Inspiration:
Exploration: Visit local street food markets to discover diverse chimichanga variations. Take note of unique fillings, sauces, and presentation styles for inspiration.
2. Interact with Street Vendors:
Exploration: Strike up conversations with street vendors to learn about their techniques, spice blends, and family traditions that contribute to their signature chimichangas.
3. Tasting Tour of Chimichangas:

- **Exploration:** Embark on a tasting tour, sampling chimichangas from different vendors. Pay attention to the subtle variations that make each one unique.

C. Tips for a Homemade Food Cart Experience
1. Set Up a Chimichanga Station:

- **Homemade Experience:** Create a DIY chimichanga station at home, allowing guests to assemble their chimichangas with various fillings, sauces, and toppings.

2. Authentic Food Cart Atmosphere:

- **Homemade Experience:** Enhance the experience by creating an authentic food cart atmosphere. Use colorful decorations, play street music, and consider using food cart-style serving containers.

3. Small Bites and Snacks:

- **Homemade Experience:** Offer smaller-sized chimichangas or chimichanga bites for a more snackable experience, reminiscent of street food offerings.

Recreating the street food adventure at home involves capturing the essence of authenticity, exploring local markets for inspiration, and infusing the homemade experience with the vibrancy and flavors of street-style chimichangas.

Chapter(16) Dessert Chimichangas

A. Sweet Filling Options
1. Banana-Nutella Delight:

- **Sweet Filling:** Fill tortillas with slices of banana and a generous spread of Nutella for a delicious combination of creamy chocolate and sweet banana.

2. Apple Cinnamon Bliss:

- **Sweet Filling:** Sauté diced apples with cinnamon, brown sugar, and a touch of butter. Use this warm mixture as a sweet and comforting chimichanga filling.

3. Strawberry Cheesecake Indulgence:

- **Sweet Filling:** Combine cream cheese with fresh strawberries and a hint of sugar. Use this luscious mixture as a filling for a strawberry cheesecake-inspired dessert chimichanga.

B. Decadent Chocolate Varieties
1. Triple Chocolate Sensation:

- **Decadent Chocolate Filling:** Combine dark chocolate, milk chocolate, and white chocolate chips as the filling. The result is a gooey and indulgent triple chocolate experience.

2. Chocolate and Peanut Butter Delight:

- **Decadent Chocolate Filling:** Mix melted chocolate with creamy peanut butter for a rich and satisfying filling. Add chopped peanuts for extra crunch.

3. Salted Caramel Chocolate Drizzle:

- **Decadent Chocolate Filling:** Melted chocolate combined with a salted caramel drizzle creates a heavenly filling. Sprinkle sea salt on top for an irresistible sweet-savory balance.

C. Serving with Ice Cream and Dessert Sauces
1. Vanilla Bean Ice Cream Topping:

- **Ice Cream Pairing:** Serve dessert chimichangas with a scoop of vanilla bean ice cream for a classic pairing that adds a cool contrast to the warm and crispy chimichangas.

2. Cinnamon Sugar Dusting:

- **Dessert Sauce Enhancement:** Dust chimichangas with a mixture of cinnamon and sugar. Drizzle with chocolate or caramel sauce for an extra layer of sweetness.

3. Berry Compote Drizzle:

- **Dessert Sauce Enhancement:** Create a berry compote using a mix of strawberries, blueberries, and raspberries. Drizzle over the dessert chimichangas for a fruity and tangy twist.

Dessert chimichangas offer a delightful and creative way to satisfy your sweet tooth. Experiment with various sweet fillings, decadent chocolate varieties, and serving options to create a memorable and indulgent dessert experience.

Chapter(17) Seasonal Chimichanga Creations

A. Springtime Freshness

1. Asparagus and Lemon Zest Filling:

- **Springtime Freshness:** Celebrate spring with a filling of sautéed asparagus spears and a sprinkle of fresh lemon zest. The bright and vibrant flavors capture the essence of the season.

2. Pea and Mint Infusion:

- **Springtime Freshness:** Create a refreshing filling by combining sweet peas with mint. The combination adds a burst of flavor and a touch of elegance to your spring chimichangas.

3. Radish and Avocado Salsa:

- **Springtime Freshness:** Top your spring chimichangas with a salsa made from diced radishes, avocado, cilantro, and lime juice for a crisp and flavorful accompaniment.

B. Summer BBQ Twist

1. Grilled Corn and Black Bean Filling:

- **Summer BBQ Twist:** Embrace the flavors of summer with a filling of grilled corn and black beans. Add a hint of smokiness by charring the corn on the barbecue.

2. Pineapple Habanero Salsa:

- **Summer BBQ Twist:** Create a spicy and sweet salsa using diced pineapple and habanero peppers. This bold topping adds a tropical kick to your summer chimichangas.

3. BBQ Pulled Pork Delight:

- **Summer BBQ Twist:** Use succulent BBQ pulled pork as the filling for a hearty and satisfying chimichanga, perfect for summer gatherings.

C. Fall Harvest Flavors
1. Butternut Squash and Sage Filling:

- **Fall Harvest Flavors:** Embrace the bounty of fall with a filling of roasted butternut squash and fresh sage. The earthy and sweet notes capture the essence of the season.

2. Apple Cider Reduction Drizzle:

- **Fall Harvest Flavors:** Drizzle chimichangas with a reduction of apple cider, cinnamon, and a touch of maple syrup for a cozy and autumnal flavor profile.

3. Pumpkin Pie Chimichangas:

- **Fall Harvest Flavors:** Create a dessert chimichanga with a pumpkin pie-inspired filling, complete with pumpkin puree, spices, and a graham cracker crumb crust.

D. Winter Comfort Chimichangas
1. Braised Short Rib Filling:

- **Winter Comfort:** Fill chimichangas with braised short ribs for a rich and comforting winter experience. The slow-cooked meat adds warmth and depth of flavor.

2. Cranberry and Brie Topping:

- **Winter Comfort:** Top winter chimichangas with a decadent combination of cranberry compote and melted brie for a sweet and savory twist.

3. Hot Chocolate Dessert Chimichangas:

- **Winter Comfort:** Indulge in a dessert chimichanga filled with a gooey chocolate and marshmallow mixture, reminiscent of a comforting cup of hot chocolate.

Seasonal chimichangas allow you to embrace the flavors of each season, from the freshness of spring to the cozy comfort of winter. Tailor your fillings, toppings, and accompaniments to reflect the best of each season's bounty.

Chapter(18) Kids in the Kitchen

A. Child-Friendly Recipes
1. Cheesy Chicken and Rice Chimichangas:

- **Child-Friendly Recipe:** Create a filling using shredded chicken, rice, and melted cheese. Kids can easily assemble these simple yet delicious chimichangas.

2. Peanut Butter Banana Dessert Chimichangas:

- **Child-Friendly Recipe:** For a sweet treat, spread peanut butter on tortillas, add banana slices, and fold into chimichangas. Bake until golden for a delightful dessert.

3. Mini Veggie Quesadilla Chimichangas:

- **Child-Friendly Recipe:** Make mini chimichangas with a veggie-loaded filling. Kids can customize their creations with colorful vegetables and cheese.

B. Creative Chimichanga Shapes
1. Pinwheel Chimichangas:

- **Creative Shape:** Roll out tortillas, spread the filling, and roll them into pinwheels before frying. Kids will love the spiral shape and the surprise inside.

2. Animal Face Chimichangas:

- **Creative Shape:** Use cookie cutters to shape tortillas into animal faces. Fill with a child-friendly filling, fold, and secure with toothpicks before frying.

3. Letter or Number Chimichangas:

- **Creative Shape:** Cut tortillas into letter or number shapes. Kids can create their names or spell out words with the filled and folded chimichangas.

C. Cooking as a Family Activity
1. Chimichanga Assembly Line:

- **Family Activity:** Set up an assembly line with different filling options, sauces, and toppings. Each family member can contribute to the chimichanga-making process.

2. Chimichanga Decorating Contest:

- **Family Activity:** Turn chimichanga-making into a friendly competition. Family members can compete to create the most visually appealing and delicious chimichanga.

3. Storytime and Cooking:

- **Family Activity:** Combine storytelling with cooking. Share stories about the origins of chimichangas or create a family tale while preparing and enjoying the meal together.

Involving kids in the kitchen fosters a love for cooking and provides an opportunity for creativity and bonding. Child-friendly recipes, creative shapes, and family cooking activities make the chimichanga-making experience enjoyable and educational for everyone.

Chapter(19) Culinary Crossroads: A Vegetarian Journey

A. Showcasing Plant-Based Innovations
1. Jackfruit Carnitas Filling:

- **Plant-Based Innovation:** Showcase the versatility of jackfruit by preparing a filling that mimics the texture of carnitas. Season with smoky spices for an authentic flavor.

2. Mushroom Walnut Taco Meat:

- **Plant-Based Innovation:** Create a savory and umami-filled filling using a combination of finely chopped mushrooms and walnuts. The mixture resembles traditional taco meat but is entirely plant-based.

3. Cauliflower Al Pastor:

- **Plant-Based Innovation:** Experiment with cauliflower marinated in al pastor spices for a flavorful and satisfying vegetarian filling that pays homage to traditional Mexican cuisine.

B. Vegan Chimichangas
1. Vegan Cheese and Black Bean Delight:

- **Vegan Chimichanga:** Combine vegan cheese with black beans, corn, and spices for a hearty and delicious vegan chimichanga filling.

2. Chickpea and Spinach Fusion:

- **Vegan Chimichanga:** Sauté chickpeas and spinach with garlic and cumin for a protein-packed and nutritious vegan chimichanga filling.

3. Sweet Potato and Black Bean Medley:

- **Vegan Chimichanga:** Roast sweet potatoes and mix with black beans, creating a sweet and savory vegan chimichanga filling. Add spices like cayenne for a hint of heat.

C. Exploring Tofu and Tempeh Options
1. Tofu Scramble Breakfast Chimichangas:

- **Tofu and Tempeh Exploration:** Scramble tofu with turmeric, peppers, and onions for a breakfast-inspired chimichanga that's both satisfying and plant-based.

2. Soy-Lime Tempeh Fajita Filling:

- **Tofu and Tempeh Exploration:** Marinate tempeh in a zesty soy-lime mixture and grill with fajita-style vegetables for a flavorful and protein-rich chimichanga filling.

3. General Tso's Tofu Chimichangas:

- **Tofu and Tempeh Exploration:** Create a fusion-inspired chimichanga by coating tofu in a sweet and spicy General Tso's sauce before baking or frying.

Exploring plant-based innovations, crafting vegan chimichangas, and experimenting with tofu and tempeh options offer a delicious and sustainable approach to the culinary world. These vegetarian alternatives showcase the diverse and satisfying possibilities that can be achieved without meat.

Chapter(20) Culinary Arts and Plating Techniques

A. Presentation as an Art Form
1. Colorful Palette Plating:

- **Artistic Presentation:** Use a vibrant array of ingredients and garnishes to create a visually stunning and colorful palette on the plate. Consider contrasting hues for an eye-catching display.

2. Layering for Depth:

- **Artistic Presentation:** Experiment with layering components to add depth to your presentation. Place chimichangas on a bed of rice, surrounded by colorful salsas and sauces, creating a visually appealing composition.

3. Edible Flower Accents:

- **Artistic Presentation:** Garnish with edible flowers to add a touch of elegance and sophistication to the plate. Choose flowers that complement the flavors of the chimichangas for a cohesive presentation.

B. Creating Instagram-worthy Dishes
1. Top-Down Photography:

- **Instagram-Worthy Technique:** Capture the beauty of your chimichangas by taking top-down photos. This perspective showcases the layers and textures, making it visually appealing for social media.

2. Play with Angles:

- **Instagram-Worthy Technique:** Experiment with different angles to find the most flattering shot. Capture close-ups of the golden crispiness or a side profile highlighting the fillings.

3. Background Contrast:

- **Instagram-Worthy Technique:** Choose a background that contrasts with the colors of the chimichangas. A neutral or complementary background allows the dish to stand out and grab attention.

C. Food Styling Tips from Professionals
1. Saucing Techniques:

- **Professional Food Styling**: Use a squeeze bottle or a small spoon to apply sauces with precision. Create elegant swirls, drizzles, or dots to enhance the visual appeal of the dish.

2. Microgreens and Herbs:

- **Professional Food Styling:** Sprinkle microgreens or finely chopped herbs around the plate's edges for a polished and restaurant-quality look. These small details add freshness and color.

3. Clean Plate Technique:

- **Professional Food Styling:** Wipe the edges of the plate to ensure a clean presentation. This attention to detail creates a professional and sophisticated appearance for your chimichangas.

Mastering the art of presentation and incorporating professional food styling techniques can elevate your chimichangas from a delicious meal to a visually stunning culinary masterpiece. Whether you're aiming for an artistic presentation or creating Instagram-worthy dishes, attention to detail and thoughtful styling make a significant impact.

Chapter(21) The Science of Perfect Chimichangas

A. Understanding Cooking Chemistry
   1. Maillard Reaction for Flavor Development:

- **Cooking Chemistry:** Utilize the Maillard reaction by ensuring proper browning of the tortilla during frying. This chemical process enhances the flavors, creating a complex and savory profile.

2. Leavening Agents in Dough:

- **Cooking Chemistry:** If making your own tortillas, understand the role of leavening agents like baking powder. Proper ratios contribute to the desired texture and thickness of the tortillas.

3. Oil Absorption Dynamics:

- **Cooking Chemistry:** Understand how oil absorption works during frying. Maintaining the right temperature is crucial for achieving the ideal crispiness while preventing excess oil absorption.

B. Achieving the Ideal Crispiness
1. Temperature Control for Frying:

- **Ideal Crispiness:** Maintain a consistent frying temperature. Too low a temperature results in oil-soaked chimichangas, while too high a temperature may burn the outer layer before the inside is cooked.

2. Double-Frying Technique:

- **Ideal Crispiness:** Consider the double-frying technique. After an initial fry, let the chimichangas rest before a second, shorter fry. This method enhances crispiness by ensuring thorough cooking while maintaining a crispy exterior.

3. Draining Excess Oil:

- **Ideal Crispiness:** After frying, place chimichangas on paper towels to drain excess oil. This step is crucial for preserving crispiness while preventing them from becoming greasy.

C. Mastering the Art of Flavor Balance
1. Seasoning Throughout the Layers:

- **Flavor Balance:** Ensure a balanced distribution of seasoning throughout each layer. Season the filling, coat the tortilla, and consider seasoning the exterior for a harmonious flavor experience.

2. Acidic Components for Brightness:

- **Flavor Balance:** Incorporate acidic components like lime juice or vinegar to add brightness to the flavors. This helps cut through the richness, providing a well-balanced taste.

3. Umami-Rich Ingredients:

- **Flavor Balance:** Introduce umami-rich ingredients such as soy sauce, mushrooms, or aged cheeses to enhance the depth of flavor. Umami contributes to a more satisfying and savory experience.

Understanding the cooking chemistry behind chimichangas, achieving the ideal crispiness through proper frying techniques, and mastering the art of flavor balance are key elements in the science of creating perfect chimichangas. These insights allow you to take a more intentional and informed approach to crafting this beloved dish.

Chapter(22) The Future of Chimichangas

A. Emerging Trends and Innovations
  1. Plant-Based Revolution:

- **Trend Prediction:** Expect to see an increase in plant-based chimichangas with innovative fillings, showcasing the evolving trend toward more sustainable and plant-centric diets.

2. Global Fusion Influences:

- **Trend Prediction:** Anticipate the incorporation of diverse global flavors and techniques, such as Asian, Middle Eastern, or African influences, leading to exciting fusion chimichanga variations.

3. Smart and Functional Ingredients:

- **Innovation:** The use of smart and functional ingredients, such as gluten-free flours, ancient grains, and nutrient-dense options, will likely become more prevalent, catering to health-conscious consumers.

B. Predictions for Chimichanga Evolution
1. Tech-Infused Cooking:

- **Prediction:** The integration of technology, including smart kitchen appliances and cooking apps, could revolutionize the chimichanga-making process, making it more accessible and user-friendly.

2. Personalized Chimichanga Experiences:

- **Prediction:** With a growing emphasis on personalization, expect to see customizable chimichanga experiences at restaurants and food establishments, allowing customers to tailor fillings, toppings, and sauces to their preferences.

3. Elevated Culinary Experiences:

- **Prediction:** Chimichangas may move beyond casual fare, with chefs elevating the dish in upscale restaurants. Fine dining interpretations of chimichangas with premium ingredients and intricate plating could become a culinary trend.

C. Reader Contributions and Recipes
1. Share Your Chimichanga Creations:

- **Reader Contributions:** Readers are invited to share their chimichanga recipes and innovations. Whether it's a unique filling, a creative fusion twist, or a family tradition, these contributions will add a personal touch to the future of chimichangas.

2. Innovative Techniques from Home Cooks:

- **Reader Contributions:** Home cooks can contribute innovative techniques they've discovered, whether it's a unique way to fold chimichangas, a special seasoning blend, or a time-saving kitchen hack.

3. Culinary Traditions and Stories:

- **Reader Contributions:** Share culinary traditions and personal stories related to chimichangas. Whether it's a cherished family recipe passed down through generations or a memorable chimichanga experience, these stories enrich the cultural tapestry of this beloved dish.

The future of chimichangas holds exciting possibilities with emerging trends, technological advancements, and the creativity of home cooks and chefs alike. Reader contributions will play a significant role in shaping the evolving landscape of chimichanga recipes and experiences.

❖ Conclusion

A. Recap of Key Concepts

In this culinary journey exploring "Chimichanga Creations: A Flavorful Journey into Mexican Cuisine," we've covered a diverse array of topics, from the history and significance of chimichangas to kitchen essentials, classic recipes, creative variations, healthier alternatives, and beyond. Let's recap the key concepts that make chimichangas a fascinating and versatile dish:

- **Historical Roots:** Chimichangas have a rich history, and their significance in Mexican cuisine reflects the blending of flavors and culinary traditions.
- **Kitchen Essentials:** Equipping yourself with the right tools, essential ingredients, and tips for success is crucial to mastering the art of chimichanga making.
- **Creative Variations:** From seafood and vegetarian options to breakfast chimichangas, exploring creative variations allows you to tailor this classic dish to diverse tastes and preferences.
- **Healthier Alternatives**: Baked chimichangas, lean protein options, and whole grain wrappers offer healthier alternatives without compromising on flavor.

- **Sides and Accompaniments:** Elevate your chimichanga experience with the perfect salsa, guacamole, rice and beans pairings, and refreshing salads.
- **Expert Tips:** Insights from Mexican chefs provide invaluable advice, secret ingredients, and personal touches that enhance the authenticity of your chimichangas.
- **Celebrations:** Chimichangas aren't just a meal—they're a celebration. From festive occasions to customizing for special events and hosting chimichanga parties, there are endless ways

to enjoy and share this culinary delight.

B. Encouragement to Explore and Experiment

As you embark on your chimichanga culinary adventures, remember that the joy of cooking lies in exploration and experimentation. Don't be afraid to add your own twist to traditional recipes, try new fillings, or venture into uncharted flavor territories. The kitchen is your creative canvas, and chimichangas provide a versatile platform for your culinary expression.

C. Final Thoughts on the Versatility of Chimichangas

In conclusion, chimichangas stand as a testament to the incredible versatility of Mexican cuisine. From the classic flavors rooted in tradition to innovative, contemporary twists, chimichangas adapt to a myriad of culinary preferences. Their ability to blend flavors, textures, and cultural influences makes them a beloved and enduring dish.

So, whether you're savoring a traditional chimichanga, exploring global fusion variations, or crafting your own unique recipe, remember that the journey into the world of chimichangas is as delightful as the dish itself. May your chimichanga creations bring joy to your table and continue to be a source of culinary inspiration. ¡Buen provecho!